1/11 CP

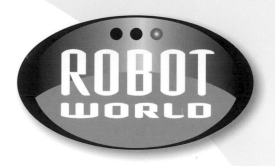

ROBOT
WORLD

● **Robots**
in Space

by Steve Parker

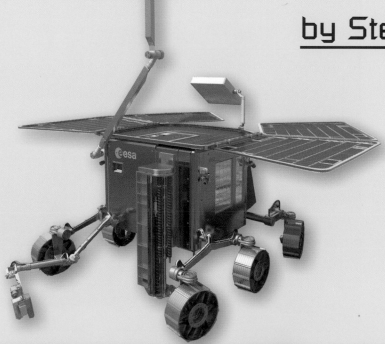

amicus

Published by Amicus
P.O. Box 1329
Mankato, MN 56002

Printed in the United States of America, at
Corporate Graphics in North Mankato, Minnesota.

Library of Congress Cataloging-in-Publication Data
Parker, Steve, 1952-
  Robots in space / by Steve Parker.
    p. cm. – (Robot world)
  Summary: "Discusses how robots are used
to explore planets and other bodies in space,
advances in space robotics, and what we can
learn from the data these robots gather"–
Provided by publisher.
  Includes index.
  ISBN 978-1-60753-075-6 (lib. bdg.)
  1. Space robotics–Juvenile literature. I. Title.
TL1097.P37 2011
629.8'92–dc22

                              2009040657

Created by Appleseed Editions Ltd.
Designed by Guy Callaby
Edited by Mary-Jane Wilkins
Picture research by Su Alexander

Picture acknowledgements
title page ESA; contents ESA/D.Ducross; page 4 NASA-MSFC;
5 RIA Novosti/Alamy; 6 NASA-AMES; 7l NASA-Ames Research
Center/Eric James, r NASA-HQ-GRIN; 8 NASA/JPL-Caltech/
University of Arizona/Science Photo Library; 9t Detlev Van
Ravenswaay/Science Photo Library,b NASA/Science Photo
Library; 10 ESA, Image by C. Carreau; 11 NASA-JPL; 12t Peter
Arnold, Inc/Alamy, b NASA/JPL; 13 Warren Kovach/Alamy;
14l RIA Novosti/Alamy, r NASA courtesy Northrop Grumman;
15 NASA; 16 ESA; 17 NASA-KSC; 18 NASA-MSFC; 19t RIA
Novosti/Alamy, b NASA-HQ-GRIN; 20 ESA/D.Ducross;
21t Chris Butler/Science Photo Library, b NASA-JPL; 22t JAXA,
b Johns Hopkins University Applied Physics Laboratory/
Science Photo Library; 23 Detlev Van Ravenswaay/Science
Photo Library; 24 ESA-NASA; 25t ESA/D.Ducross, b NASA;
26 NASA-JPL; 27 JHUAPL/SWRI/NASA/Science Photo Library;
28 William K. Hartmann,UCLA/NASA/Science Photo Library;
29t NASA-KSC, b NASA/Science Photo Library
Front cover NASA/Science Photo Library

DAD0040
32010

9 8 7 6 5 4 3 2 1

Contents ●

Robots Blast Off!

Very few people go into space. To become an astronaut, you have to train for years. It must be amazing to look down on planet Earth spinning slowly below, and to look up at distant planets, moons, and stars. But robots do this every day!

Space shuttles carry satellites and other space robots into space.

ROBOT OR NOT?

Rocket-bot?

*Is a space rocket a robot? Not really. It can travel, has moving parts, and controls itself to some extent. But we call rockets launch vehicles rather than true robots. We use the word robot to describe some of the machines that rockets carry, such as wheeled **rovers** or remote-control **landers** that touch down on a planet.*

Danger, Danger!

Space is a dangerous place. There's no air to breathe, no food or drink—in fact, nothing at all. Traveling somewhere interesting, such as a planet, takes months or even years. If you were to get there, it might be too cold or hot to survive. If your spacecraft breaks down, help is a long way away.

Equipped to Cope

None of this worries a robot. Most robots are machines made of metals, plastics, and similar materials. They don't need air, water, or food, although they do need energy to keep them going—usually electricity. They have no feelings, so they don't feel lonely or frightened.

Small and Simple

A spacecraft carrying people needs food, drinks, and other supplies. It must have safety equipment and backup systems. The craft has to be able to withstand enormous heat as it re-enters the **atmosphere** (the thick layer of air around the Earth) to bring the astronauts home. A spacecraft carrying a robot needs no supplies. It can be smaller and lighter, so it needs a smaller rocket for liftoff, and it costs less too.

ROBOT SUPERSTAR

Lunokhod 1

The first robot to land on another world was Lunokhod 1 *from Russia. It was carried by the spacecraft* Luna 17 *and touched down on the moon in 1970. It was 7.5 ft. (2.3 m) long and had eight wheels and two TV camera eyes. Guided from Earth by remote control,* Lunokhod *was a great success. In 11 months it traveled more than 6 miles (10 km) and took 20,000 pictures.*

On Earth and in Space

Are space robots the same as robots on Earth? In many ways, yes. Most robots are partly automatic. They can make simple decisions and work on their own for a time. Most robots have parts that move, such as levers and motors. Some can travel on wheels or bendy legs. All these features make them ideal for work in space.

Robots Need People

Robots carry out tasks for us. They may be very smart, especially the latest types with computer "brains." But they cannot work on their own all the time. They need instructions or programs from us; otherwise they do not know what to do. Also something might happen that a robot is not programmed to deal with. Then a person has to take control of the robot and decide what to do.

Robots designed to drill into the Moon or Mars are tested in the bone-chilling cold of the Arctic region.

Robots in Action ■

TESTED TO THE LIMIT

Compared to our planet, on other worlds the conditions such as temperature and air pressure are much more extreme. Test versions of space-bots are taken to the coldest and hottest places on Earth to see if they work well. This can reveal possible problems such as frozen wheels or overheated motors. ■

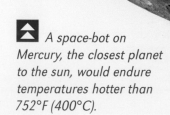
The K10 Mars rover can "see" into the ground with its very powerful radar that uses strong radio waves.

Emergency Repairs

When a robot breaks down on Earth, someone can usually repair it, but if a robot breaks down in deep space, there will be no one around to fix it. So space-bots must be designed very carefully. They need lots of backup equipment and reserve systems to make sure that if one part fails, another can take over. They have to be tested in the most extreme conditions they might encounter.

DO YOU KNOW?

(ROBOTS DO)

How Much Do Robots Cost?

It's difficult to say how much space robots cost. There's the cost of the robot itself, including its design, development, and testing. There's also the cost of the launch rocket, and the control and communications center here on Earth. For the two Mars rovers Spirit *and* Opportunity *(see page 17), the total was about $410 million each. That's cheap compared to sending people into space, which would cost hundreds of times more!*

A space-bot on Mercury, the closest planet to the sun, would endure temperatures hotter than 752°F (400°C).

● Electro-bots

Most robots are powered by electricity. But in deep space, there are no electrical outlets where we can plug in a robot to recharge its batteries. So how do space robots keep going?

Using Electricity

Electricity is the most convenient way to power a robot. Most robots store instructions and information in microchips and memory discs powered by electricity. Electricity also drives the motors that move the robot's parts. But space travel can last for months or years and even the most powerful batteries would run down. So space robots must be able to recharge their batteries.

Power from the Sun

Robots that are not too far from the sun can use its light to make electricity. They have **solar panels** very similar to the panels we use on Earth, which capture the energy in sunlight and turn it into electricity. These panels are big, to catch enough light. They are usually folded up while the robot is launched into space. Once the robot is in space, the solar panels open.

ROBO-FUTURE

Help for Earth

*Every year, scientists make solar panels that are better, or more efficient, at turning sunlight into electricity. This research helps space robots—and also improves the way we use solar power here on Earth. If we make electricity using solar power, we can make less electricity by burning **fossil fuels** in power plants. So using solar power helps to combat **global warming**.*

◀◀ *After the Phoenix lander touched down on Mars in May 2008, it opened its solar panels, which are about the same size as a double bed.*

 *Mars is farther from the sun than we are, so the sun looks smaller and dimmer from there. Scientists need to allow for this when they design solar panels for Martian space-bots.*

Deep Space Darkness

Away from the sun, beyond the planet Mars, the sunlight is too weak to charge solar panels. So deep-space robots have a device called an **RTG**. The initials stand for radio-isotope thermoelectric generator. This machine uses a specially-made lump of a radioactive substance for fuel, such as **plutonium**. It gives off rays and radiation that warm sets of wires made of different metals, called **thermocouples**. The heat makes electricity flow through the wires to charge the batteries. RTGs can produce (or generate) electricity for years at a time.

ROBOT SUPERSTAR

Pioneer 11

Pioneer 11 *was launched in 1973 on an immensely long journey past the giant planets Jupiter and Saturn, and on into deepest space. Its radio signals continued for more than 22 years until its four shoebox-sized SNAP-19 RTGs finally became too weak to make enough electricity.*

Senses in Space

We send space robots on great journeys for many reasons. We want to discover what other worlds are like, such as distant planets or moons. Is the surface covered with diamonds? Are there aliens? Could people survive there? To send us the information we want, space robots need **sensors**. They have cameras to see, microphones to hear, "hands" to touch and feel, and other sensing devices.

Space Science

Space robots don't go on trips just to satisfy our curiosity. Scientists want specific information about other worlds, such as the temperature there, what the surface rocks and dust are like, and whether there is any air. This information helps them understand how planets, stars, and other objects formed long ago, and how they might end in the distant future.

In 2008, deep-space traveler Rosetta *passed near the asteroid Steins and took pictures with its telescopic and wide-angle cameras (see page 23).*

What Do Robots See?

Nearly all space robots have a camera. In fact, most have more than one. Many of these cameras take still pictures. Others record videos or movies. The digital cameras change the patterns of light rays into electronic digital codes and send these to Earth by radio waves. Some cameras look through telescopes to get close-up views. Others have wide-angle lenses to show the bigger picture.

 *Outermost planet Neptune has been visited only once, by* Voyager 2 *in 1989. The space probe sent back wonderful color pictures of this mysterious deep-blue world.*

What They Measure

Space robots have many other sensors besides cameras. Thermometers check the temperature, **gravity** detectors measure the force (or pull) of gravity, radio receivers record natural radio waves sent out by stars, and **magnetometers** measure the magnetic forces around a planet or moon. All this scientific information helps us to understand more about space and about our own planet Earth.

 *In 1995, the* Galileo *robo-craft mapped the giant planet Jupiter, taking pictures with infrared light that our own eyes cannot see.*

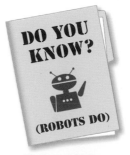

DO YOU KNOW?

(ROBOTS DO)

Robot Vision

*Human eyes can't see the types of light called **ultraviolet** or **infrared**. But many space robots can. They have special cameras that take pictures using these types of light rays. Computers can then turn the information into pictures human eyes can see.*

Talking to Space-bots

The fastest speed in the universe is the **speed of light**, which is 186,000 miles (300,000 km) per second. The radio signals we send and receive from space robots are similar to light rays, and they travel at the same speed. But space is so vast, even that's not fast enough.

Robo-comms

We use radio communications to talk and listen to space robots. Scientists send them instructions as radio signals telling them what to switch on and turn off, where to point their cameras, and where to go. The robots send information back to Earth about what their cameras see and all the things they measure.

▼ *As space robots journey to the edge of our solar system, radio signals take several hours to travel to and from Earth. This is called communication lag.*

Be Careful

For some space robots, the time delay causes problems. It's not possible for someone on Earth to drive a robot rover on Mars by remote control. If the person sees through the camera that the rover is heading for a rock, and steers away, the rover would hit the rock before it got the signal to turn. So robot rovers explore very slowly. Some have touch sensors to feel objects and a computer that recognizes anything that might be in the way.

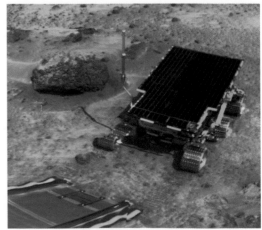

▶▶ *The* Sojourner *rover on Mars used laser beams to detect things in its path (see page 17).*

A Long Delay

Here on Earth, distances are so small that radio signals bring TV shows to your antenna or dish in fractions of a second. Signals take about 1.25 seconds to travel to the moon. Mars is a lot farther. Even when it is nearest to Earth in its **orbit** (journey around the sun), radio signals take more than 5 minutes to travel there. When Mars is on the other side of the sun from us, signals take more than 20 minutes. Signals to and from the *Cassini* robot probe, which is going around the distant planet Saturn, take more than an hour to arrive.

ROBO-FUTURE

Subspace Messages

Scientists have many ideas about whether some kinds of rays or waves could travel faster than light. If so, they would make "subspace" communications possible, so that radio signals traveled along them in just seconds rather than hours.

▶▶ *Giant radio dishes receive the amazingly weak signals from space robots and radio back instructions to them.*

Robots in Action■

IN A SPIN—RADIO SILENCE

Planets and moons spin around at different speeds. A space robot on another world faces away from Earth for half the time and we do the same as Earth turns. These times are "radio blackouts" because radio signals, like light rays, cannot curve around a planet. The space-bot cannot send us information or receive our instructions.■

Off to the Moon

Some people love the idea of visiting another world, such as the moon or Mars, to live there for a time. Before humans could build a living base there, we would have to send robots to find a good site and check for problems.

Wrong Place!
Even touching down on another world is very dangerous. You might land on a steep cliff, a big boulder, or in a pile of deep dust. It's best to send a robot scout to find the safest landing area before people travel there.

Looking Up-Close
The *LRO*, or *Lunar Reconnaissance Orbiter*, is a robot **satellite** that travels around the moon studying its surface. Its powerful telescope cameras photograph mountains and valleys, cliffs, boulders, and flat dusty plains in great detail. *LRO* can look into craters to detect any signs of frozen water, which would be very useful for people living in a moon base.

▼ *In 1976,* Lunar 24 *brought samples of moon dust and rock back to Earth.*

Crash Photos
LCROSS is a special robot that watched a space rocket plunge to its death! It was launched by the same rocket as LRO and its cameras saw the rocket smash into the moon at more than 5,590 mph (9,000 km/h). Scientists can study pictures of the explosion, the crater it made, and the dust it threw up, to learn more about the moon's surface.

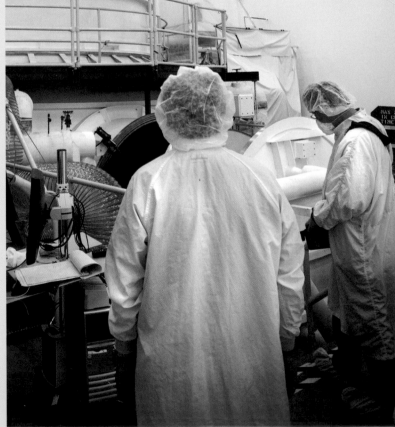

⬆ *This version of* Scarab *is a prototype, or trial model. It's for testing on Earth in moon-like places such as soft sand, steep hills, and boulder-covered plains.*

Scouting Around

Another moon robot is *Scarab*, a four-wheeled rover the size of a sports car. There is plenty of sunshine on the moon, but *Scarab* is designed to explore deep, dark craters, so it has an RTG for electricity (see page 9). It can find its own way using laser beams and an onboard computer—and it can drill! It can lower itself down onto its underside and send a drill 3.3 ft. (1 m) down into the rocks, to look for ice, water, minerals, and any other useful substances.

ROBOT OR NOT?
○○○

Sat-bot?

Is a satellite in space a robot? In most cases, not really. It does a simple job for us, such as beaming down TV signals or taking photographs. But a satellite does not usually have moving parts, and it is not programmed to make decisions for itself, whereas many space robots are.

Let's Go to Mars!

Mars is the most visited place in space after our moon. More than 40 robot craft have passed nearby, gone into orbit, or landed on the surface of the red planet. But Mars is also a risky place to visit. More than half of all Mars missions have run into trouble or failed completely.

The European Space Agency (ESA) plans to launch the ExoMars mission in 2013. The ExoMars rover will search for water and other signs of life on Mars.

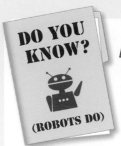
Lost Forever?

Late in 2003, the Mars lander Beagle 2 *left its orbiting **mothercraft**,* Mars Express, *and headed down to the surface. Then all radio contact was lost. No one knows whether it landed or not, or if it was destroyed.*

Failure, Success

The first space robots to land on Mars were *Mars 2* and *Mars 3* in 1971. But scientists on Earth lost radio contact with them as they touched down. Much more successful were the *Viking 1* and *Viking 2* landers in 1976. They couldn't move around, but they had cameras and other sensors, including wind and earthquake detectors. They carried out chemical tests to see if there was any life, but they found nothing.

Roving Around

In 1997, *Mars Pathfinder* sent down a lander that released a skateboard-sized robot rover, *Sojourner*. The rover spent three months exploring Mars, photographing the rocks and scenery, and analyzing the soil (see photo on page 12). Once again, it found no Martian life. Like many other robot space rovers, *Sojourner* finally lost all electrical power. It's still there on Mars, silent and still and "asleep."

Ice on Mars

The *Phoenix* lander arrived on Mars in May 2008. It was the size of a small truck, with big solar panels, springy legs, and equipment to measure the weather, soil, and rocks. It found evidence of water ice on Mars. Although this doesn't prove there is life on Mars, water is one of the things required for life. Scientists are looking for other areas of ice on Mars. *Phoenix* finished its mission in November, when there was no longer enough sunlight for its solar panels.

▼ *Nine-year-old Sofi Collis won a competition to name the two Mars rovers, with her suggestions of* Spirit *and* Opportunity. *Before that they were called* MER-1 *and* MER-2.

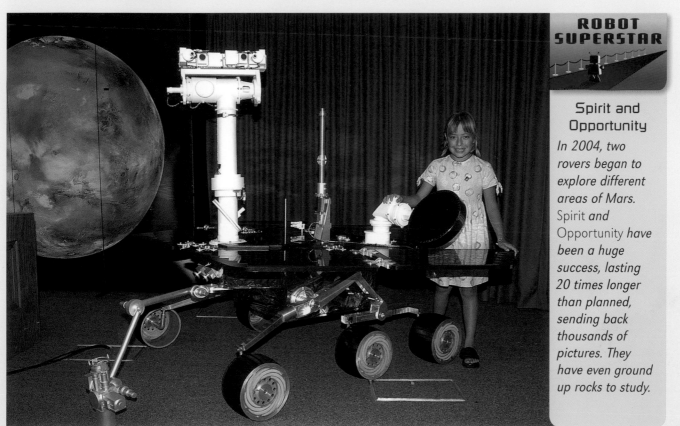

ROBOT SUPERSTAR

Spirit and Opportunity

In 2004, two rovers began to explore different areas of Mars. Spirit *and* Opportunity *have been a huge success, lasting 20 times longer than planned, sending back thousands of pictures. They have even ground up rocks to study.*

Red-Hot Planets

The closest planet to Earth is Venus. It's a mysterious world, covered in thick clouds of poisonous gases and acid drops. Humans could never survive there, and even space robots have problems.

Hotter than an Oven

The temperature on Venus is 860°F (460° C), more than twice as hot as an oven. The thick gases of the atmosphere on Venus have a pressure almost 100 times the **air pressure** here on Earth. So this planet has presented a huge challenge to space robot designers.

Through a telescope, the planet Venus looks like a giant swirling blob. Space robots have traveled down to see its rocky, mountainous surface.

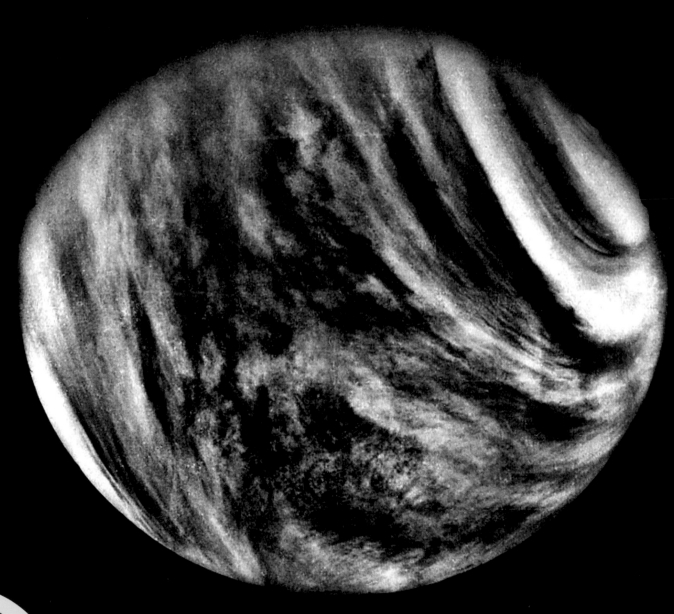

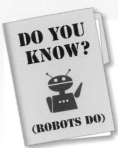
Mystery Loss

The first robot spacecraft to reach the surface of another planet was Venera 3 *in 1966. At least, that's what scientists think. Radio contact was lost as it arrived. So it was probably damaged by a crash landing. But who knows what really happened?*

Many Visitors

From the 1960s to the 1980s, a long series of *Venera* robot probes touched down on Venus and sent back pictures and other information. In 1978, the *Pioneer Venus Multiprobe* included five mini-robots. The *Magellan* space-bot orbited Venus from 1989 to 1994 and *Venus Express* arrived in 2006. Both of these have **radar** equipment that can see through the thick clouds to map the surface.

Almost on Fire

Mercury is the closest planet to the sun, and its surface temperature reaches 806°F (430°C). It has only been visited once by a robot space mission, *Mariner 10,* in 1975. A second robot visit is planned by *Messenger,* which was launched in 2004 and should arrive in 2011. That's a very long time to travel to a relatively close planet. This is because Mercury is so near the sun that the sun's huge gravity tries to pull a space robot into its fiery surface. So *Messenger* has to approach very carefully and use its **thrusters** to brake hard and slow down.

SOHO, the Solar and Heliospheric Observatory, has 12 measuring instruments that study the hottest object around—the sun, whose surface is 10,832°F (6,000°C).

ROBOT OR NOT?

Floating Robots

In 1985, the Vega *mission sent two landers to Venus, and also two balloons! Each balloon was about 11.2 ft. (3.4 m) across and floated for more than 40 hours through the thick* **acid clouds**. *Their equipment measured temperature, wind speed, and pressure. Are such balloons true robots? Their official name is autonomous flying robots or aerobots.*

Exploring Together

Many space missions involve not just one robot, but two or more working as a team. A common combination is an orbiter and a lander. The orbiter goes in circles around the planet or moon, and releases the lander to touch down on the surface.

Seven-Year Trip

The greatest robot team so far to explore space is *Cassini* and *Huygens*. They set off together in 1997 to the giant planet Saturn with its beautiful rings. They took almost seven years to reach Saturn's orbit. In early 2005, the lander *Huygens* left the **orbiter** *Cassini* and plunged toward the surface—but not Saturn's surface. Its target was Saturn's massive moon Titan.

Huygens' heat shield glowed as it hurtled down into Titan's atmosphere, then fell away. Two parachutes, one after the other, slowed it down further. Huygens landed at a speed of 16 ft (5 m) per second—about as fast as a human runs.

Massive Moons

Space scientists are always planning the next mission for their robots. They plan to launch Europa Jupiter Mission System *in 2020 to the biggest planet, Jupiter, to explore its four massive moons Io, Europa, Ganymede, and Callisto.*

Only One Window

Like Titan, *Cassini* orbits around Saturn. Space scientists had to make sure that *Cassini*, Titan, and *Huygens* all moved into the best positions for the landing. There was only a short time period (or "window") during which this could happen, as with many space missions. A mistake would have spelled disaster for the robot team.

Hero Huygens

Huygens was a heroic space-bot. For two and a half hours, it plunged through the atmosphere of Titan, protected by a heat shield and slowed by two parachutes. During the descent and for 90 minutes afterward, it sent back more than 350 pictures by radio, as well as information about Titan's winds, weather, and icy surface. Small *Huygens* sent radio signals to bigger *Cassini*, then *Cassini's* more powerful radio equipment sent them on, or relayed them, all the way back to Earth.

⬆ Huygens' *target was Titan, here on the right, with ringed Saturn in the background. Titan is so huge that it has its own atmosphere. Parachutes only work if there is an atmosphere.*

⬇ *The orbiter* Cassini *has taken thousands of pictures of Saturn and its moons Titan (three views are shown below), Rhea, Iapetus, and others. Its mission will last at least 14 years.*

Small Strange Worlds

Asteroids and **comets** are other objects space robots might visit, and they have their own special hazards. Asteroids tumble and turn as they zoom through space, so it's difficult to land on them. Comets grow very hot when they're near the sun and squirt out powerful, volcano-like blasts of gases.

Soft Landing

Asteroids are chunks of rock traveling around the sun that are too small to be planets. Various robot craft, such as *Mariner 9, Galileo,* and *Deep Space 1,* have flown near asteroids and photographed them. The first to go very near an asteroid was *Near Earth Asteroid Rendezvous—Shoemaker,* usually called *NEAR-Shoemaker.* It was launched in 1996, flew close to asteroid Mathilde in 1997, then orbited and finally soft-landed on asteroid Eros in 2001. It took pictures and made measurements for about two weeks before it went to "sleep."

▼ *Robot craft* NEAR-Shoemaker *approaches asteroid Eros, preparing to touch down. Finding Eros in the vast depths of space was an amazing feat—it is just 18.6 mi. (30 km) long.*

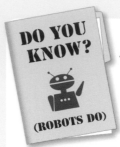
Trouble in Space

A deep space robot called Hayabusa *has had troubles on its travels. It set off in 2003 to land on the asteroid Itokawa and gather samples of rock and dust to bring back to Earth. But its 3.9 in. (10 cm) mini-lander drifted away, its balancing equipment broke, its thrusters jammed, and its landing went wrong. Scientists hope it may still come back to Earth, but no one knows yet whether it has any samples.*

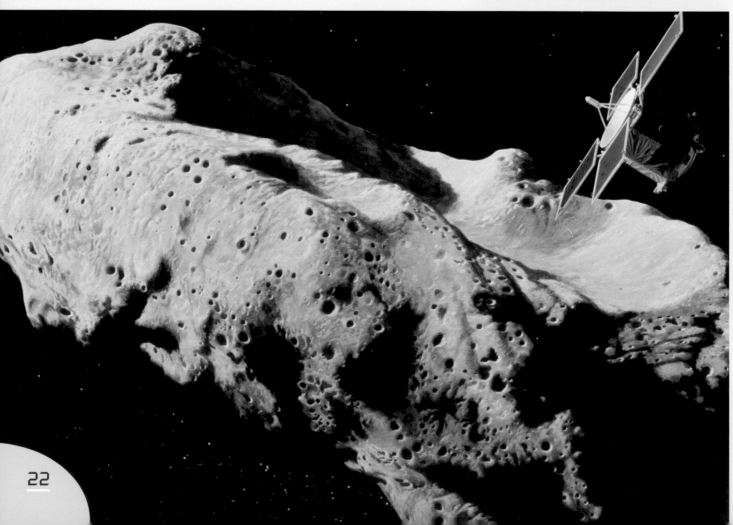

Not So Soft

A space robot made a far harder landing on a comet five years later. Comets are balls of ice and dust that come from far outside the planets, loop around the sun and head away again, glowing as they pass. In 2005, Comet Tempel 1 came quite close to Earth, so space robot *Deep Impact* went to meet it. After studying and photographing it, *Deep Impact* released a section called an impactor that slammed into Tempel 1, causing an explosion equal to one made by igniting five tons of dynamite. *Deep Impact* and telescopes here on Earth recorded the collision to find out what comets are made of.

◄◄ *The refridgerator-sized impactor from* Deep Impact *made a crater 109 yd. (100 m) wide in Comet Tempel 1. The comet flashed briefly, shining six times more brightly than usual.*

ROBO-FUTURE

Far into the Future

In 2004, the mothercraft Rosetta *(see photo page 10) and its robot lander* Philae *took off for Comet Churyumov-Gerasimenko. It's a long trip, and they should arrive in 2014. On the way, they are flying past asteroids Steins (visited in 2008) and Lutetia (2010).*

International Space Station

Not all space robots go on long journeys among the planets. Some stay quite close to Earth and do regular jobs, such as taking supplies to the the International Space Station.

Space Ferries

The International Space Station—or ISS—orbits about 217 miles (350 km) above Earth's surface, going once around the planet every 91 minutes. Spacecraft such as *Soyuz* and space shuttles carry people to and from it. There are also ISS robo-ferries, or space trucks. These are robotic craft that work on their own, with no crew. They are launched by rockets and fly to the ISS with food, water, fuel, tools, and scientific equipment. These robots also take new parts so that astronauts can continue building the ISS, which will not be finished for several years.

▼ *Building work on the ISS, codenamed Alpha, began in 1998. Dozens of robot craft have carried up new parts to attach to it.*

Only Used Once

The most regular robot ferries are Progress freighters. They are similar to the *Soyuz* craft which has carried crew members up into space and back for many years. About four Progress craft go to the ISS every year. They are always new, because they are destroyed once they have completed their tasks. Each craft travels to the ISS with more than two tons of supplies and automatically attaches itself or docks to the ISS. It is unloaded and then filled with waste. Then it leaves the space station, heads back to Earth, and burns up on re-entry into the atmosphere.

Auto Space Truck

In 2008, another automatic space truck joined the ISS team. This is the **ATV**, or Automated Transfer Vehicle. It is bigger than a Progress freighter and has up to ten tons of supplies and a complicated computer that controls its approach and docking with the ISS. Like Progress, every ATV self-destructs—it burns up on its way back to Earth.

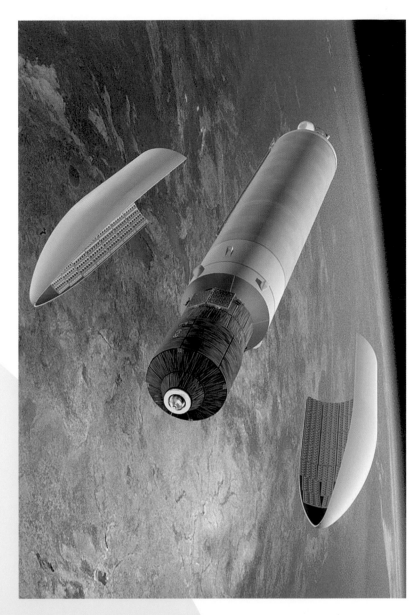

▶▶ *The* Ariane 5 *rocket's nose opens to release the ATV robot ferry on its way to the ISS. Its cargo includes food, water, oxygen, thruster fuel, clothes, and science experiments.*

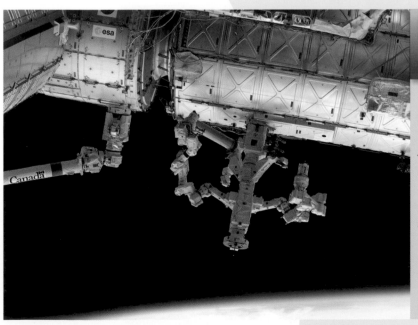

ROBOT SUPERSTAR

Dextre

In 2008, a two-armed robot called Dextre *was sent to the ISS. Its full name is the Special Purpose Dexterous Manipulator (SPDM). It has two movable arms, each more than 10 ft. (3 m) long, and a 10-foot (3-m) long body. The arms have hand-like grabs that bend and twist.* Dextre *stays outside the ISS and carries out tasks such as adding on new pieces brought by Progress and ATV. This means human crew members do not have to take a spacewalk outside.*

The Longest Journey

Pluto is a long, long way away from Earth. This **dwarf planet** is at the edge of the solar system and has not been visited by any space robots—yet. The greatest robo-traveler of our time, *New Horizons*, is on its way there.

Even seen through a very powerful telescope, Pluto looks tiny from Earth. It is just one object in the vast jumble of stars and planets.

DO YOU KNOW?

(ROBOTS DO)

Fastest Ever

New Horizons *zoomed away from Earth at more than 36,000 mph (58,000 km/h). It was the fastest object ever to leave our planet.*

Endless Mission

New Horizons left Earth in January 2006. Just over a year later, it had passed Jupiter. Then in 2008, it whizzed past Saturn's orbit. But Pluto is so far away that it won't arrive there until 2015. After studying the dwarf planet and its big moon Charon, *New Horizons* will go on, and on, as long as scientists on Earth can track it and stay in contact.

Waiting and Waiting...

New Horizons is almost the size of a car and has a very big radio dish. Eventually it will be so far from Earth that its radio signals will become very weak, and they will take four hours to arrive here. Its five packs of equipment include a powerful telescope camera, a close-up camera, and a dust collector. Like all deep-space robots, *New Horizons* has an RTG to make its electricity (see page 9).

New Grows Old

New Horizons is on such a long journey that by the time it reaches Pluto in 2015, it will seem old and out of date. Scientists started building it in 1998 and spent years designing and testing it. In the meantime, technology on Earth advances almost every week, as computers grow faster and more powerful. Space scientists need to make sure that the latest equipment here can still receive signals from space robots that were built ten or even 20 years ago.

▲ *As* New Horizons *flew past Jupiter, it took close-up pictures of the planet and many of its moons, including hundreds of active volcanoes on the moon Io.*

Robots in Action ■

SLEEP TIME

On some parts of a space robot's long journey, there is little for it to detect or measure. Keeping all of its equipment working would waste power. Many of its circuits and systems are shut down and the space-bot goes "to sleep." As the next important stage approaches, it receives wake-up signals from Earth. ■

Infinity and Beyond

Space scientists are never short of ideas for new robots and other craft that will go faster, travel farther, take more pictures, and gather more information about our world and the universe.

On its Way

The *DAWN* space robot is aiming for several firsts. It will be first to visit the asteroid Vesta and the dwarf planet Ceres (formerly called an asteroid) in the asteroid belt between Mars and Jupiter. This is a very long way away. *DAWN* blasted off in 2007, but will not reach Vesta until 2012 and Ceres until 2015. *DAWN* has special new engines called xenon ion thrusters. Usually robotic spacecraft that visit two places simply fly past the first, without going into orbit. But *DAWN* will use its **ion engines** to power out of orbit around Vesta and head on to Ceres.

▲ *DAWN's main body or "bus" is about the size of a small car and its radio dish is about 5 ft. (1.5 m) across. It measures almost 65 ft. (20 m) in length, including its solar panels.*

Stardust

In 2006, Stardust *returned to Earth's orbit after a journey of seven years and 3.1 billion miles (5 billion km). This space robot had a part which looked like a big, sticky tennis racket that folded out as it whizzed past Comet Wild 2, to collect tiny bits of space dust from the comet. The dust samples came back to Earth's surface in a re-entry container that landed by parachute.* Stardust *continued into deep space. It showed that deep-space "sample return" missions can be successful, and now more are planned.*

◀◀ Stardust *is prepared for launch in 1999. The brown and white cake-like part on top is the return capsule that landed back on Earth.*

Robo-astronaut

Most space robots look nothing like humans because they are designed to do jobs that humans can't do. *Robonaut* is human-shaped, with movable arms and hands, and five fingers. It has been designed to take over tasks once carried out by astronauts in spacesuits. Each arm and hand has more than 150 sensors for touch, position, and temperature, as well as for force of movement and grip.

▶▶ *Robonaut is an android, which means it's a robot with a human-like shape.*

The Smartest Yet

Several space robots have searched for life on Mars without success. Could ExoMars *find it? This robot space probe will have an orbiter, a lander and a rover similar to* Spirit *or* Opportunity. *The* ExoMars *rover will be the most intelligent space-bot ever, able to find its own way, steer around obstacles, and "sniff" for signs of life. But it will not be ready for a long time—its launch is planned for 2013.*

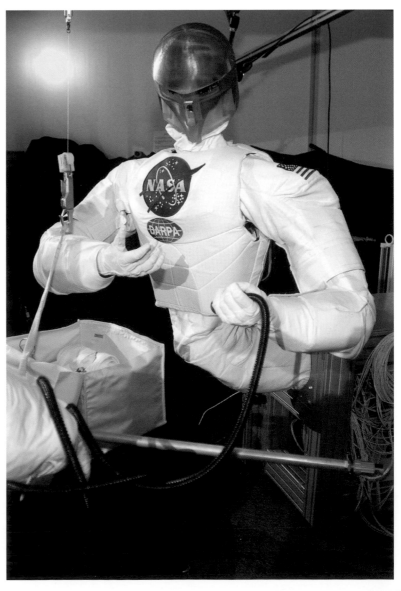

Glossary

acid clouds
Clouds made of tiny floating drops of acid chemicals, which burn and eat away things they touch.

air pressure
The pressing force of the invisible floating gases in the air or atmosphere around us on Earth.

asteroid
A large lump of rock in space traveling around the sun, which is not big enough to be a proper planet and which does not give off gases, unlike a comet.

astronomer
A scientist who studies stars, planets, and other objects in space.

atmosphere
The layer of gases around a large space object such as a star, planet, or big moon. It usually grows thinner the higher it is above the surface.

ATV
Automatic Transfer Vehicle, a robot spacecraft that travels from Earth with no crew to join the International Space Station.

comet
A lump of mixed rock, dust, and ice in space going around the sun, which gives off gases and dust when it is warmed near the sun.

dwarf planet
A lump of rock in space which is too small to be a proper planet but too large to be an asteroid.

fossil fuels
Substances we burn for heat, which are the preserved remains of plants and other living things from millions of years ago. The main ones are coal, oil, and natural gas.

global warming
The gradual heating up of Earth due to increasing amounts of certain gases in its atmosphere, especially carbon dioxide, which is produced by burning fossil fuels and other fuels.

gravity
The natural pulling force that all objects have, from pieces of dust to stars, that attracts other objects. The bigger or more massive an object, the stronger its gravity.

infrared light
Light with waves slightly longer than red light waves, which our eyes cannot see, but which some cameras and other sensors can detect.

ion engine
An engine similar to a rocket engine but much weaker, which uses electrical and magnetic forces to move tiny particles called ions and cause a push or thrust.

lander
A spacecraft designed to touch down or land without damage on another world (planet, moon, asteroid, or comet) and carry out measurements and experiments.

magnetometer
A device that measures the magnetic field or magnetic force around an object, from a simple fridge magnet to a whole moon, planet, or star.

mothercraft
A larger spacecraft to which a smaller craft or probe is attached. It usually carries the smaller craft to a certain place and releases it for its mission.

orbit
Going around and around a larger object on a regular path or track.

orbiter
A spacecraft designed to orbit a large space object such as a planet, moon, asteroid, or comet, rather than fly past it or land on it.

plutonium
A rare heavy metal substance that gives off rays and radiation, including heat rays.

radar
Sending out radio signals and detecting them when they bounce back off an object, to show the size, shape, and distance of the object.

robot probe
A robot craft without a crew that carries out a task in space.

rover
In space exploration, a vehicle or buggy that moves around under its own power, usually on wheels.

RTG
Radio-isotope Thermal Generator, a device that makes electricity from heat, using a substance such as plutonium for fuel.

satellite
An object that goes around, or orbits, another one. The moon is a natural satellite of Earth. Often the word is used to mean man-made objects rather than natural ones.

sensor
A device that detects and measures something, such as a camera for light, a microphone for sound, and a magnetometer for magnetic forces.

solar panels
Large flat surfaces containing many small electrical gadgets called solar cells that turn light energy into electricity.

speed of light
About 186,000 miles per second (300,000 km/s), the fastest speed in the universe, not only for light but for radio waves, X-rays, and similar rays and waves.

thermocouples
Lengths of wires of different metals joined together end to end, through which electricity flows when they are heated.

thrusters
Small rocket-like engines that puff out spurts of gas to make a spacecraft twist around or change its position.

ultraviolet light
Light with waves slightly shorter than violet light waves, which our eyes cannot see, but which some cameras can detect.

Further Reading

Davis, Barbara. *The Kids' Guide to Robots.* Kids' Guides. Mankato, Minn: Capstone Press, 2010.

Hyland, Tony. *Space Robots.* Robots and Robotics. Mankato, Minn.: Smart Apple Media, 2008.

Jefferis, David. *Space Probes: Exploring Beyond Earth.* New York: Crabtree Publishing, 2009.

Miller, Ron. *Robot Explorers. Space Innovations.* Minneapolis: Twenty-First Century Books, 2008.

Siy, Alexandra. *Cars on Mars: Roving the Red Planet.* Watertown, Mass.: Charlesbridge, 2009.

Strom, Laura Layton. *From Bugbots to Humanoids: Robotics.* Shockwave. New York: Children's Press, 2008.

Web Sites

Cassini Equinox Mission
Get all the latest updates from NASA about what space robot Cassini is discovering about Saturn and its moons. The site also includes details of the spacecraft, classroom materials, recent images taken by Cassini, and more.
http://saturn.jpl.nasa.gov/index.cfm

ESA—The Aurora Project
The official site of the European Space Agency's future robotic mission to Mars details the progress of the mission and describes the ExoMars robot.
http://www.esa.int/esaMI/Aurora/index.html

NASA Robotics—Robotics Alliance Project
Read about how NASA is using robotics to plan future space exploration missions. Sections for students and educators suggest robotic projects for the classroom.
http://robotics.nasa.gov/index.php

● Index